Cityscapes of the USA

Cityscapes of the USA

Avery Nightingale

Contents

1

Introduction

A cityscape is defined as the physical aspect of an urban area. Thus, cityscapes, it would seem, are characterized by buildings only. In fact, a cityscape can consist of the people themselves (the people in a bustling metropolis "make" that city) – and a cityscape can certainly be of the non-physical kind as well; for example, the cityscape of Paris is in many minds associated with seduction, Amsterdam with drugs, or New York with crime. To be sure, the so-called "city of love" has a large number of beautiful buildings – and to many people that is a part of its cityscape – but other people are not very interested in the cityscapes at all.

Cityscapes are important, though. They not only serve as the physical frame of our lives, but in western culture, have also served at various times and in various ways as identity markers. In this essay, the cityscapes of the USA will interest me. The United States of America is a diverse country; it is home to people of many different religions, ethnicities and cultural backgrounds. This is reflected in the cityscapes of the USA – the cityscape of New York is different from that of Palmyra in Missouri where only 730 people live; where the only two buildings are long abandoned; and where the sign above the front gate of the town says "Population 730/Expect a Miracle." In this essay, we will look at the cityscape of Chicago;

discuss the revitalization of commercial streets in the postindustrial city; give quantitative descriptions of several cities; and recount Fred's and Frank's views of Los Angeles.

2

Historical Evolution of American Cities

The United States of America is renowned for her vibrant and diverse cities. America is the third most populous country in the world - home to over 300,000,000 people - and the vast majority of these live in urban areas. Every visitor to the United States is likely to spend time in at least a couple of cities. The cities presented in this course, with the notable exception of Santa Fe, are the country's major urban centres with populations ranging from 600,000 people in Boston, Massachusetts up to 8.4 million in the "Big Apple" - New York City. American cities are popular because of their sights and attractions, the architecture, museums and parks, musical events, and drinking and eating emporia. This suite of resources sets out to explore America's urban gems: and also to understand and explain how and why these cities have evolved into the spaces they are today.

The cities explored are almost all former European colonies (Chicago only becoming established in the early Nineteenth century). The age and historical development of these cities varies between regions. The oldest American city explored in this topic is Boston founded in 1630; the newest is Los Angeles (founded in 1781, but didn't approach its present size until the Twenties). The formation and transformation of these urban systems were affected by a number of external political, social, economic and physical factors beyond their control. This section of the suite gives a broad historical overview of the development of American cities, presenting the context to the two parts that follow. These detail the rise of the "Northeast Megalopolis" (Washington • Baltimore • Philadelphia • New York • Boston) and the "Pacific Rim" Cities (Seattle - Portland - San Francisco).

3

Architectural Styles Across US Cities

From the painted Victorian houses of San Francisco to the Spanish Colonial style of the Southwest, through the Back Bay's Italianate brownstones in Boston, cities in the United States often showcase a hodgepodge of architectural styles that have graced the country since its founding. Long before European colonization, Native American buildings varied by tribe and culture. The United States boasts a rich architectural heritage, thanks to the wide variety of immigrants who settled throughout the 19th and 20th centuries. Prior influences, such as French and Spanish colonizers, influenced tastes in the American South and Southwest, while Italian immigrants inspired much of the architecture in Portuguese in New England, according to Brigid Daniel with the Encyclopedia Britannica. The result is a nation of cities boasting architectural styles not often seen outside of their birthplaces. Here are five unique buildings, and tips for exploring them.

Neoclassical grandiosity, Art Deco sleekness, and new buildings reflecting modern infill trends all grace the City of Brotherly Love, and much of this walking tour is dedicated to commingling the oldest and newest architecture. Philadelphia is one of the best, and first, places to experience Colonial architecture in the United States. William Penn, founder of the city in 1681, was unlike his predecessors in Massachusetts: He didn't want to duplicate British society, and wanted to design a grid city full of broad, leafy streets and public squares, designed by architect Thomas Holme. Before long, a second generation of Philly's colonial era nabobs looked to express themselves through brick and stone construction rather than wood, and created a style known as Georgian. Geometrically precise and highly symmetrical, Georgian homes — think tall and narrow with stolid brick faces, windows evenly bribing three stories, pediments above driven-centered doors — reflect the balance and order popular in early American society.

4

Urban Planning and Development

The urban towns and cities in the USA came into existence through the slow process of planned development and the prolific imagination of industry leaders. These towns and cities have developed based on organized systems and principles that ensure continuity and systematized development of an urban area. The main feature of these planned development towns and cities is the allotment of land in an organized and systematic manner, typically defined by a grid pattern, wide streets, and roads. In diverse American towns and cities, there is a systematic development of the commercial part of town and the rectangular plat system, as it is more commonly known. The purpose of the platting is to ensure ease of development and transfer of properties and to systematize the urban space.

Urban planning, land reclamation, and the development of waterfronts are one of the major responsibilities for any city throughout the United States. City council, developers, and other stakeholders spend a lot of time in planning and re-planning cities and their waterfronts. Some cities, such as Chicago, have benefited from their positioning and natural water resources, having been used to dig a canal to connect the Great Lakes to the Mississippi River in the 19th Century. Its natural waterways have now been modified to create a network of waterways and lakes. Furthermore, Chicago has landlocked industries that encourage the development of water transport to import and export goods around Park. Other cities actively seek to add water to their land, perhaps by using land-fill to extend the land area around the edges of the city. The main reason is to attract people to the city by adding new amenities. Whether created through planning or accretion, the new waterfront must incorporate specific processes to effectively manage and develop the land for cultural, historical, recreational, and commercial purposes.

5

Cultural Diversity in Urban Centers

Cultural diversity is the beating heart of many U.S. cities. Urban life, more than anything else we encounter as we travel, defines what it is to be an American in a modern context. The proportions of foreign-born residents, ethnic culture, and, hardest of all to peg down, the feel of a place – from the neon twinkling of immigrant businesses to the crowds washing over the street during a cultural festival are all vital measures of the deeply ingrained ethnic identity winding its way through a given neighborhood.

But perhaps the most genuine means of approximating the experience of being in foreign lands can be found in cities like New York, San Francisco, Chicago, and even the inner suburbs of cities like Los Angeles and Miami, where a confluence of urbanity and multiple cultures combine to create a rich, multicultural experience. Immigrants from the U.S.'s European diaspora, like Greeks in Lynchburg, Va., Poles in South Bend, Ind., and Ukrainians in Parma, Ohio, have created the feel and character of cities far from home. These urban oases give the foreign traveler a wholly American experience. This international experience is not just limited to the old neighborhoods of the old cities, where local branches of the fraternal order of Sons of Norway still hold elaborate socials. Every city's old foreign population has exported its own mix of geography, culture, and color, creating a multi-ethnic landscape from the street to the silhouette. Long before it became a hallmark of '80s liberal bumper sticker car culture, "diversity" has been the modus operandi of U.S. urban centers across the country. Long ago, thousands of miles from home, an avid traveler and Sicilian-speaking American would have found solace in San Francisco, New York, or New Orleans. Though the language and cost of admission may have changed, cities still offer a tantalizing taste of the abroad, at close to home.

6

Economic Significance of American Cities

American cities are among the largest and most important places of their kind in the world. American cities are commercial cities, where most of the economically active population is in commerce or manufacturing services. The United States' Gross Domestic Product (GDP) in 2020 is forecasted at almost US$22 trillion. The country has the planet's biggest economy, accounting for some 25% of world GDP. Cities such as New York, Los Angeles, Chicago, Houston, San Francisco, Dallas, Miami, etc. are economic powerhouses that derive much wealth and prosperity, and generate considerable jobs, by the many large corporations that are headquartered or have substantial operations there. Many are the headquarters cities of multinational corporations and major banks. New York is the world's leading financial center, including trading in foreign exchange and commodities, and in the 1980s was a major recipient of eurocurrency bank deposits; Los Angeles, Detroit, and Philadelphia have giant motor vehicle and chemical manufacturing sectors; and Detroit, Cleveland, and Pittsburgh are steelmaking centers. City-region economies vary greatly. Boston's financial services and its concentrations in biotechnology, life sciences, and information technology have made its regional economy boom. Houston is perceived as the world's energy capital because it is home to about 4,600 energy-related firms with shares listed on the stock exchanges, including 23 of the world's largest firms. Tourism is an important economic activity for sun-belt cities. Overall, the rest of the world needs these commercial cities because they still manufacture or extract many types of secondary goods that are in demand in other countries and at relatively low cost. Reno and Las Vegas attract significant numbers of international visitors, many partially drawn by their reputation as inexpensive places to marry. Many cities in Florida attract wealthy people from all parts of the world because they are wonderful places in which to retire.

Economic factors drive urban growth, and its benefits include wage increases and productivity gains. The size of the expansion of a city's economy is defined by the elasticity of city wage at population size. Big cities are economically diversified because of the different labor force they offer. Big cities cover the costs of congestion through real wages that are higher than elsewhere. In a very big city, workers favor a 1% increase in nominal wages to a reduction by 1% of congestion. However, real wages rise with the average wage level in the city. Productivity in cities tends to rise faster than the main idea suggests - the standard deviation of productivity is proportional to 1/2 times the labor force remaining in the city, while the proportion of spatial agglomeration remains higher than zero. Nevertheless, the number of big cities is being reduced by the forces of sinking. The reasons people congregate at some city locations and not at others can partly be explained by the degree of spatial agglomeration. One would reason in an area with positive spatial agglomeration that eagerness for individuals to be in the same place is rising with the number of others who are present. In such an area, it can be expected that companies exist in which more workers should be working for those companies and not less, as workers are attracted to the degree of spatial agglomeration. Officially, the degree of spatial agglomeration is calculated from the increase in population density.

7

Innovations and Technologies Shaping Urban Spaces

The innovations that are taking place in cities across the United States are informed by the technologically advanced industrial and post-industrial history of the nation. At present, the USA is shaped by a history of a car-focused city planning paradigm, automobiles, and a strong automobile industry, and this is still evident in the design and function of many American cities. For example, St. Paul's bicycle shares are automated and require no employees to uphold the business model. They are also powered by solar panels. Additionally, the Brightline in Miami uses Adaptive Cycle Software designed by Railpoint. This software helps make service to service changes more efficient.

In addition to innovations in transportation in cityscapes, advancements in architecture, design, waste management, and the use of space are clearly shaping current cityscapes in the USA. Various technologies and design places are shaping current cityscapes in the USA. Many of these innovations are influenced by the history of city developments in this region that were designed or altered to favor the automobile. However, buildings are adapting or being built to be more environmentally friendly. They are often hosting plants or are described as having "living walls." Waste management in this region also embraces technology as the Trashbot goes around and picks up the garbage. Smart street furniture is also beginning to pop up in cityscapes. These designers and creators are striving to produce aesthetically pleasing and energy-efficient design allowing a large number of people to gather and feel welcomed.

8

Sustainable Urban Development Practices

American cities are champions of fast-paced, sustainable urban development. Environmental factors play a crucial role in the planning and development processes, and many cities have already gone a step further by involving local communities to adopt historically and culturally accurate urban planning guidelines that suit their situations.

Local community involvement may involve residents and businesses at annual public gatherings to develop guidelines for developing conceptual ideas about neighborhood designs during busy periods. It may also provide a range of opportunities for city identification of cultural and natural assets, investment in indigenous cultural life experiences, and original attractions for new events or attractions.

Various American cities are looking at developing and promoting heritage in their future urban growth strategies. This might include the identification of appropriate principles for the design of new buildings in older suburbs, in line with heritage-place design indicators.

Furthermore, the planning and development of states and cities on the west coast of the United States (Los Angeles, San Francisco, California, etc.) have often included environmental design and high-quality, attractive architecture. It is part of their "stock-in-trade", not a "niche-market" product.

Just as every sustainable urban development agenda throughout the United States cannot fit into considered and concise guidelines, the following "features" may help define some of the action. Every sustainable urban process that involves economic asset management, environmental stewardship, and the conservation of resources, or a holistic combination of these, can be included. It may reflect their goals and practical realization, as suggested, as well as the nature, depth, range, and requirements of local solutions for cooperation with neighborhoods and local committees/people to implement those standards.

There are principles and practice directions focusing on environmental elements, resource-friendly management, and community involvement.

9

Case Studies of Iconic American Cityscapes

Denver, Colorado/Nadia M. Anderson Historic American town: Flagstaff, Arizona/Jessica Godinez and Taylor Haid Iconic Miami: Reflecting the American Dream/Terri L. Voepel Portland, Oregon: An evolving post-industrial urban landscape/ Lori R. Davis San Francisco's waterfront: A palimpsest of changing alignments/Caroline Scruggs and Vanessa Fernandez-Sosa San Francisco's Chinatown: City under the city/Khyaati Chattopadhyay and Karen Robertson Utica, New York: The city that once was and is yet to be/Dorthe H. Bern and Laura Elen A. Mills

This book presents case studies designed to revisit simplistic ideas of iconic cityscape. This term, 'cityscape', remains elusive and has seemingly lost its usefulness. Moreover, scholars have argued that iconicity has been over-extended during the past two decades as a result of the processes of globalization, to the extent that we must look beyond merely iconic representations to analyze cityscapes. To remedy these deficiencies, the book raises a number of critical questions: How do we analyze built environments to reveal multiple narratives regarding identity and belonging? What is the impact of globalization on architectural and interpretive sensibilities and on what used to be known as a city? How can analyses of architectural history help us to comprehend cultural and economic processes, to contextualize architectural styles as well as urban spaces, and to understand the concomitant aesthetics of laissez-faire capitalism? (excerpt)

10

The Future of American Cityscapes

The past, present, and future of urban America have been shaped by an ever-evolving set of processes. Urbanization and the growth of American cities have driven the rise of cityscapes, both as physical landscapes and as cultural symbols. Although a bevy of forces has coalesced to create contemporary American cityscapes, there are several likely scenarios that may define new cityscapes in the future. The time-space dilemma, in particular, will be increasingly shaped by advancements in information technology and data privacy. As urbanites continue to compress time, reducing webs of interconnectedness into instantaneous existence, serious ethical questions regarding the data trails left behind since our urban renaissance will continue to be asked.

Both population and economic activity are increasingly concentrating in and around urban spaces. However, looking ahead, just what kind of urban centers America is home to may change. The increasing interconnectivity of twenty-first-century global civil society, the rise of emerging megacities, and the declining manufacturing base for many long-standing brownfield urban cores will affect the dynamics and scale of the urban landscape and the positioning of the U.S. within this metropolitan world order. Future developments, from climate change to global political conflict, are only likely to increase the urgency of addressing and preparing for existential challenges that confront not only city residents but the entire world population.

11

Conclusion and Reflections

In our exploration of American cityscapes, we have sought to provide travelers, both from within the nation and from without, with an overview of some of the country's best-known urban gems, revealing a slice of the lauded American way of life. From Miami to San Francisco, we have learned that US cities present a striking diversity both of people and landscapes, and this insight sheds light into the heart of what it is to be an American, making these discussions of more than mere passing interest. These discussions are, we hope, also an inspiration to escape the familiar haunts of cities like New York, even if just by a mile. Whether in the Midwestern heartland or on the two great coasts, every city has its particular charm. Indeed, the researchers embarked on the present book knowing nothing about Newark, Norfolk, or even Pawtucket, and leave with an enhanced appreciation of these seemingly quiet corners of the world.

There are many reasons why out-of-towners might want to familiarize themselves with cities known first and foremost to those within them. For one, transplanted as so many of us are within the US, how much of American life is each of us really part of, and how could a customs broker in Nogales so easily fathom the workings of, say, a vermin officer in Providence? Nor can such familiarity suffice for the seeker visiting the continent for the first time. While everything in some streets of Los Angeles, for instance, has in principle been seen in movies, it is the living place that has been cradled by dreams, ravaged by flames, and so on that is the thing to see. The Book That Is Before You! We are three researchers at the City College of New York's Graduate Center (CUNY).